What Men Won't tell You

Women's Guide to Understanding Men

Table of Contents

Introduction

Women are often regarded as the mysterious gender, with intricacies and secrets that only they would ever know or understand. While this may be true in many aspects, men also have their own quirks and secrets that make them just as mysterious and difficult to comprehend for those of the opposite gender. These differences between men and women are not always communicated properly or recognized as essential to smooth, viable relationships, and may lead to issues and various conflicts later on.

Throughout history, the divide between men and women has always been controversial. Roles have been set, reversed, changed, and restructured for both the male and the female in society. In ancient cultures, men were often regarded as the leaders and protectors, while females were to be the keepers of the house. Changing attitudes in much of modern society have also transformed the roles that both men and women have, and these changes have brought about the need to understand each other even more.

In relationships, constant communication and cooperation are necessary to maintain mutual trust between both parties. If you are a woman in a relationship with a man, how you understand your partner's way of thinking will also help you to evaluate how you manage or respond to his daily reactions or responses to circumstances, whether these circumstances involve your relationship as a couple, your family, or other people or situations around you.

Are you having a hard time figuring out why your spouse, boyfriend, or partner handles an issue or responds to a person the way he does? The confusion may be because you have not fully realized just how different the male psyche is compared to the female's. These differences, after all, are what make both men and women so interesting and attractive to each other in many ways, but an improper understanding and appreciation for the male and female structures can also lead to problems.

Males and females have had to grow together and adapt to changing environments since the beginning of time. Thousands of years ago, the first human tribes spent much of their day hunting for food and gathering supplies, and men and women had to do this side-by-side. Promiscuous behavior and polygamy were also more accepted. As social mores developed, and as expectations for male responsibility became more clear, polygamous behavior became less of a practice.

The development of language and the power of communication via the spoken and written word gave men and women more insight into how they feel, what they aspired for, and how they longed for a better understanding of each other. Prose, literary masterpieces, and other forms of communication became part of how both genders exchanged flattery and promises of loyalty. Music and the arts also became another powerful tool that both men and women employed to reach out to the opposite gender.

History generally shows a major shift in gender roles as agriculture became a driving force around 5000 B.C., as large agricultural tools and machinery began to be utilized in large farming efforts. Because women could not compete with the size and strength of men, they became marginalized to other tasks, creating a subservient perspective that still permeates thinking in much of the world today. Men are regarded as the stronger gender, and women are relegated to lesser tasks. As marriage and family expectations also became more prevalent in societies, so did the need for women to accept lesser roles compared to the men, regarded by society as superior.

But as society has progressed, economic situations and changing mores have also pushed the boundaries between the genders even further, and today both men and women in progressive cultures enjoy much of the same liberties in educational opportunities, employment options, and the right to suffrage. As attitudes toward marriage and sexuality are evolving, so do the rules and practices in male-female relationships and how both genders relate to each other's differences.

No matter how long you have been in a relationship with your husband, boyfriend, or partner, it is impossible for you to understand every little thing there is to know about him, his background, his views on family, his attitudes towards roles in the family and the workplace, or how he deals with conflict or situations. Attempting to understand men is a continuing process that will not come to an end the moment you think you have discovered it all. It is a journey that you will have to take for the rest of your life together, with new and exciting discoveries each step of the way.

One obstacle that women often complain about when talking about understanding men is the fact that, generally speaking, men don't like to talk about their feelings and emotions too much. Women are often ready to bare their deepest perspectives, opinions, and experiences, sharing their feelings about everything from the most mundane to the very important. Men, on the other hand, usually have to be prodded and coerced into sharing their insights, making the communication more difficult.

This communication barrier can be a point of conflict if left unresolved, and while men have to understand the importance of sharing their thoughts and feelings with their wives and girlfriends, it is also necessary for women to realize that men are just not wired that way for the most part. Instead, women must also look at other nonverbal communication or signs that men also consciously or unknowingly use to convey their feelings and emotions.

Are you truly invested in the relationship with your partner, spouse, or boyfriend and really want to make it work? If the answer is yes, then a deeper understanding of men and their mysteries will make you a better-equipped and informed relationship partner, and will also help you manage those circumstances where your reaction or response would normally be different from your male counterpart.

In the next few pages, we will delve into some techniques you can use for reading into a man's mind and figuring out what he is *really* saying or *not* saying, what men really want and what attracts them, what makes them commit and what turns them off, and how you can better relate to their interests, desires, and aspirations in order to make yourself more attuned to their inner workings.

Are men hard to understand? Not really, if you take the time to know what makes them tick and how to get through to them. All you have to do is understand how men's brains and bodies are wired, and this will get you on the right path towards understanding what it is that make men the intriguing creatures that they are.

Chapter One: How To Read Their Minds

If you can master the art of reading a man's mind, then you already have one big advantage in the right direction. Remember, men won't always give you a piece of their mind or let you take a peek at what's inside, so you will have to either listen to what's being said between the lines, or look at other signals or forms of communication they may be sending your way.

Let's start with the fact that men are very visual creatures. Men are attracted to physical attractiveness first, especially at first sight. Some men are instantly attracted to a pretty face, a sweet smile, a sexy figure, or nice curves in the right places, but whatever it is that attracts them the most will also instantly distract them. There may be dozens of beautiful women around, but your man's attention will be instantly caught by someone who fits his type, and he probably won't see any of the others around, at least for a while.

You should also know that for a lot of men, physical attractiveness isn't all about just the looks. It can also be how a woman walks or carries herself with confidence, or the way she looks at him and smiles from the opposite end of a room. But in a general sense, it is visual appeal that immediately gets a man's attention, while all other considerations would follow later on.

How does this relate to you and your relationship? When you are out in public with your partner or spouse, don't feel jealous right away when his eyes wander off to an attractive woman. Keep in mind that this visual attraction is part of how men are wired. It doesn't mean your boyfriend or husband will wander off right away and flirt or cheat when his eyes see another beautiful woman. It just means he is still a visual creature whose attention is easily captured by physical attractiveness.

This aspect of the man's brain is also important for you to consider in your personal choices. Because men are drawn to physical beauty, you should also make the effort to look good for your partner knowing that this brings him much pleasure, not to mention makes him proud to show you off to the world. This in no way means you have to strive to always be perfect or set unrealistic expectations for yourself or how you look. It just means making efforts to look great for the man you are in a relationship with because you are aware that this attracts him even more to you.

Another way to read a man's mind is to read his body language, such as the position of his upper body (chest and shoulders). Men are naturally territorial, and a sure way to know whether they are really interested in talking to you is whether they have turned their chest and shoulders towards you even if they may be doing something else or talking to another person. You have the man's attention when he has his chest and shoulders pointed at you.

Can you tell the difference between a sincere smile and a half-smile? For most men, when they give you a half-smile which almost looks like a smirk or a sneer, they are probably joking with you, saying something in jest, or flirting with you. On the other hand, a sincere, warm smile means they are interested in having a conversation with you or are genuinely happy to see or talk to you. Another kind of smile - the closed-mouth half-grin from the corners of his mouth - means he is shy about something or may be hiding a surprise from you (such as a birthday gift he doesn't want you to find out about yet).

Men say a lot with their hands, but one way for you to find out if a man is seriously into you is if they offer their hand - literally - palm up, as a sign of reassurance, comfort, or letting you know their feelings for you have gone from just physical to a deeper emotional connection. Because men's and women's bodies are instinctively connected to each other, this gesture of hand-holding actually sends signals from the man's brains through his body, and transfers to yours, so you will feel how much affection the man has for you through this simple form of nonverbal communication.

Are you in a difficult situation or waiting anxiously for some big news or development that could cause major upheaval or changes in your life? When your husband or partner holds your hand and squeezes it tighter, he is telling you that he is right there with you and will stay with you through it all. Men will not always communicate this verbally, but will reassure you of their presence with a tight hand squeeze, or an arm around your shoulder or back, pulling you tight to his chest and tucking your head under his chin.

When it comes to sex, men give off plenty of nonverbal signals as well. On a primal level, men are usually the more sexually aggressive and will initiate sexual contact, and much of their body language will tell you if they have the hots for you. For instance, if a man is standing in front of you with his legs spread apart, or with his fingers on his belt or hanging off the pants pocket, he is subconsciously letting you know that there is sexual tension and he wants to focus your attention on his reproductive area.

Your husband, boyfriend, or partner may kiss you hello or goodbye all the time, but when the kiss on the mouth lingers for ten seconds or more, this is a sure sign that he has been thinking of you for a while and wants to make love to you. If you are talking to your man and he keeps licking his lips while looking at you, he is consciously or subconsciously letting you know that he is sexually hungry and you are the subject of his attention. Men will let you know through nonverbal signals like this that they are sexually aroused and want to sleep with you.

In your relationship, it is important to understand that men are highly sexual creatures, and when these nonverbal signals are being sent by your partner or spouse, you are the object of his desire and he is letting you know that no one else has his attention at the moment. On the other hand, if these gestures occur very rarely in your relationship, it may be a sign that something has gone wrong or is missing. When that sexual attraction from your man is no longer present, it could be a sign that hindrances are already blocking the relationship.

The man's brain is not always verbally expressed. As you have already read, men give off many messages through body language and gestures, so be sensitive to how your spouse or partner may be telling you something simply by the way he looks at you, positions his body towards you, or how he is touching you. You will learn a lot about a man and what he is saying just from those silent, often subtle hints of hand, eye, body, and facial gestures that reveal a lot of what he is really feeling and thinking about inside.

Chapter Two: What Men Want

What do men really want? It's a must for you to know and understand what your boyfriend, partner, or husband wants so you will also figure out why he responds a certain way, directs his energy and efforts toward a certain activity or interest, or is passionate about an aspect of his life that may not seem as important or pivotal to you. Men's wants and aspirations do not always align with the women in their lives, and if not addressed properly this can cause tension in the relationship.

Perhaps it is important to find out what men want in a relationship first, in order to gain a better understanding of other priorities of the average man. In an article for TheGoodMenProject.com, Jordan Gray detailed seven things that men look for in an intimate, romantic relationship:

- Praise and approval
- Respect
- Sexual connection
- Emotional intimacy
- Space
- Physical touch
- Security

At first glance, this list may seem like the very same things that women also look for in a relationship, which is true in a sense. However, it is the focus and direction that men utilize in attaining and looking for these relationship goals that set them apart from most women. For instance, men do not always readily admit that they need the profuse words of approval or praise from their partners, but this also helps them to feel loved and appreciated.

While it is mostly the women who constantly ask for approval or assurance with questions such as "How do I look?" or "How did I do with that dinner party?", men also need the constant approval and ego stroke from you. Did your husband or boyfriend fix the faucet leak, or set up the fence so your dogs can run around the yard? Your verbal praise and words of gratitude will mean a lot to your man, so don't hold back.

Men also need respect, and most men equate this with love. In his article, Gray writes, "If he feels like you disapprove of him, his career, or the things that he believes to be integral to who he is as a person, he will have a hard time trusting and loving you. The thought process behind that being "If she doesn't respect who I am at my core, then how can she really want what is best for me?"

Gray adds, "If a man's partner doesn't respect his path or mission in life, then he will find it very difficult to feel anything other than an anxious need to distance himself from her."

As a woman, you certainly want to be respected in the home, or your place of work or business. Your husband or boyfriend needs this respect as well, so be sure to always assure him that his business, profession, interests, and other activities are just as important to you. For most men, their sense of accomplishment comes from what they have achieved in their chosen profession or business enterprise, or in their pursuits of travel, creative arts, even hobbies. If you do not assure your male counterpart that his accomplishments are worth being noticed and respected, he will not only start to question himself, but also doubt the stability and the worth of a relationship with a person who doesn't see his pursuits as worth anything.

Men also want a fluid sexual connection with the person they are in a relationship with, and sex is actually one of the ways that men communicate to their chosen women (they are better at this form of communication too). While women would generally use verbal communication to show their affection, men use their sexual prowess, so this is something you should always remember.

A potential conflict may arise when the woman wants to connect emotionally by talking to the male partner, while the man tries to connect through foreplay and sexual activity. The woman might see this as an attempt by the man to avoid conversation and just make out, but most of the time it really is just the man initiating intimacy the best way he knows how to - through sex. In this case, the disconnect can be fixed through clear communication and a willingness by both the male and the female to find middle ground.

Because men are generally more sexual than women, you have to also accept that for your partner or husband, it may be hard to connect emotionally with you if you have not had any physical or sexual connection for some time. For example, let's say your partner was away on a business trip for a week and comes home really excited to see you. You want to talk to him about the trip and hear all the details, but all he really wants to do is cuddle and make love!

Why the different reactions? Because women connect emotionally through conversation, while men connect through sexual activity. So how can you find middle ground when this happens? Perhaps you can go ahead and enjoy the pleasure of each other's physical affection first (it's not like you won't get any pleasure from this anyway), and then in the afterglow of lovemaking you can then initiate the conversation. More than likely, because he is already sexually satisfied, your partner will be in a more conversational mood and will share his stories with you.

Interconnected with the sexual connection that men look for in their relationship is also the emotional intimacy. Society expects men to be strong and avoid showing their emotions as a sign of weakness. However, men also have the same emotional needs and feelings as their female counterparts, and while they may not be as showy in public, they will look for a partner with whom they can freely open up about their insecurities and achievements, failures and strengths, and how they feel about what is going on around them.

This emotional connection is best exemplified when you hear a woman who says, "He really opens up when it's just the two of us." Once a man has found a woman with whom he has a deep connection and sexual intimacy, he finds it much easier to open up to that partner about everything he is keeping bottled inside, allowing his spouse or partner to see a side of him that others do not readily see. So if you want to reach this level of intimate connection with your man, you have to connect with him physically first, with the assurance that you respect who he is and what he has made of himself in life.

One very important aspect you should not neglect in your relationship is the man's need for space. Many women do not understand why men would retreat into their hobbies, sports, or night-outs with their buddies, but fail to see the comparison with their own recreational activities and get-togethers with their own friends. Men also need free time and breathing room, and they are turned off from the relationship when their partner becomes too suffocating by not allowing them to enjoy their own activities.

Keep in mind that when your man asks for space, it doesn't necessarily mean he is getting tired of you or doesn't want to spend time with you any more. It just means he also wants to be able to enjoy things on his own, or he misses the company of his friends and wants to have fun with them. Women also need to realize that when they have problems or relationship issues, they are more likely to turn to family or friends and talk it over with them, while men would generally go somewhere and be alone to allow themselves to think it over.

Why do men look for all of these aspects in a relationship? Because just like women, men also look for security in their relationships, and they get this assurance when they have reached physical, sexual, and emotional intimacy with their partner, and are assured of the respect and appropriate space that they deserve. When these aspects are present in a healthy relationship, the man feels a sense of security and this greatly improves how he relates to his spouse or partner.

People often think of women as the ones with emotional needs that should be met in a relationship, but it should also be noted that men have emotional and psychological needs that must also be addressed in order for a healthy, vibrant relationship to ensue. As his partner, your role is to take the time and effort to find out how you can better relate to these emotional desires and assure your husband or boyfriend that you are aligned with his goals.

Simple ego boosts go a long way in raising your man's self-confidence and assuring him that you are supporting him each step of the way. Don't hold back with the encouragement and the words of appreciation; you never know who may or may not be giving those words to him out there, so you want him to know he's got a fan in you.

Think of how a simple encouragement might lift up his spirit especially after a particularly long day at work. It may have been all negative chatter and dismal reports in the workplace, so he will really appreciate any soothing words you can throw his way at the end of the day. Also, it's free! Positive and encouraging words don't cost a cent, so share them lavishly!

Chapter Three: Why Men Cheat

In popular culture, unfaithfulness in relationships is a popular subject matter portrayed and discussed in detail. Books, movies, television shows, newspaper and magazine articles, and other media platforms are full of insights and advice on how to know when your partner is cheating on you, how to deal with the situation, and what steps to take in the aftermath. Cheating in relationships, after all, happens all the time to so many people regardless of how long they have been together.

Perhaps you know or have heard of what seemed like the perfect couple who went their separate ways because the man became unfaithful or found someone else. It may have been friends or family members whom you've always looked up to and considered to be role models in relationships. Have you ever really stopped and considered what may have brought the problems on, and what may have been done to mitigate the situation?

Because men are visual creatures, it is easy for someone to immediately assume that when a guy cheats, it is because he found someone more physically attractive than his current partner. A lot of times, however, men are not just drawn to the younger, sexier, more beautiful woman when they cheat. For many men, it is because they are getting what they want emotionally, sexually, or psychologically from the other party.

There can be a myriad of reasons why men cheat, but the main causes usually hark back to problems within the relationship itself, or it can also be the man's predisposition or nature to cheat, perhaps because he has done it before (prior to the current relationship) and likes the thrill of it all. According to Laurie Watson, a sex therapist and host of the podcast *Foreplay,* "Cheating is a symptom generally of relational problems, and sometimes cheating is indicative of an individual's problem."

"The philandering guy who's got a girlfriend at every hotel for business, that's a different kind of cheating than the man who has an affair with his colleague," she adds.

Another marriage and sex therapist, Dr. Jane Greer, says men may cheat for so many reasons such as "the thrill of the chase and conquest, a sexual addiction, feeling that he's deprived or unhappy with the amount of sex they're having with their partner, emotionally upset and feel their needs aren't met by their partner."

It is interesting to note that while society often points at the lack of sexual satisfaction as one of the major reasons why men cheat or drift away, for many guys it is actually the deficiency in emotional intimacy that drives them to the arms of another woman. For his book *The Truth About Cheating,* marriage counselor M. Gary Neuman surveyed 200 different men, some of whom were faithful and some cheating. He found that 47% of these men cheated on their partners because they were emotionally unsatisfied.

"Our culture tells us that all men need to be happy is sex," Neuman says. "But men are emotionally-driven beings, too. They want their wives to show them that they're appreciated, and they want women to understand how hard they're trying to get things right."

As already discussed in the first chapter, men will not always verbally let you know that they need support or appreciation, but they do and they actually crave for this. "Most men consider it unmanly to ask for a pat on the back, which is why their emotional needs are often overlooked," Neuman adds. "But you can create a marital culture of appreciation and thoughtfulness — and once you set the tone, he's likely to match it."

While it is true that men are initially attracted to physical beauty, in Neuman's survey only 12 percent of the men said their other women were more attractive than their partners. "Often times, women take way too much responsibility for their cheating partner, saying, 'if I were thinner, if I were more [insert variable here]...but sometimes, truly, their partner's going through a midlife crisis or is struggling with his own mortality or is frustrated at work," Neuman explains.

If it were just about outward beauty, then men who are married or in a relationship with beautiful women would no longer cheat, right? And yet we all know this is not the case. Think of celebrities like Tiger Woods, Kobe Bryant, Hugh Grant, Eric Benet, and many more who were related to stunning, drop-dead gorgeous women and yet still somehow wandered into the arms of other women.

This is not to say that you, as a woman, should no longer make any effort to keep yourself as attractive as you can for your spouse or partner. Remember that your man wants to connect with you sexually, and keeping yourself sexually desirable for your husband is one way to let him know that you think of his needs and are willing to also fulfill his needs and desires. But you should also be careful not to set unrealistic expectations for yourself or set extremely high and unattainable standards based on misconceptions.

Both physical and emotional connection in the relationship should go hand-in-hand in order to maintain a healthy partnership. If you are serious about understanding your partner, the effort must be made to cultivate that intimacy and emotional connection that he looks for. Otherwise, if he is trying to connect with you but is failing, this may make him vulnerable to the attention and emotional availability that other women around him may be offering.

That ego boost to the male psyche may seem trivial, but it does hold a lot of truth and may just be what your husband or boyfriend is looking for. Men need that reassurance that they are still virile, attractive, and desirable, and when the flattery is coming from another woman instead of you, the chance that he will cheat on you increases. Men like the attention, for the most part, and this attention may be enough for them to start to develop a connection with that other woman.

Taking the time to really bond as a couple is of utmost importance if you are to develop that healthy intimacy. If you are both working and with hectic schedules during the week, make the most out of the weekend to just get away from it all and be with each other fully. There is nothing wrong with spending quality time with the whole family or with other close friends, but sometimes it is better to just be with each other first, as a couple, and rekindle that passion and desire that started it all. Even a simple getaway to your favorite weekend destination can do wonders for your relationship and keep you attuned to each other's desires and goals.

In this day and age of technological advances, it is very easy for cheating to take place. If you are not providing the emotional intimacy that your husband, boyfriend, or partner is craving for, there are plenty of options out there he may turn to. This is not to justify the act of cheating, of course. Cheating in a relationship is always wrong no matter what reasons may be pointed to as the catalyst for the behavior. But it is also worth looking at what brought about the behavior in the first place in order to better understand how it can be avoided.

At the same time, do not unnecessarily blame yourself also for any instances of cheating. Remember that no matter what the reasons may be, a man who cheats still made the conscious decision to cheat, and that is still the bigger fault in the equation, especially in a marriage where there is a binding legal contract and both parties are expected to be faithful.

Regardless of the lapses on anyone's part, unfaithfulness in a relationship, especially in a marriage, is never the solution. It is often just a smokescreen for other relational issues already taking place, but what cheating does is compound the problem and involve other parties in the situation. For what it is worth, men should not be held to a lower standard especially when entering into a commitment such as marriage.

Chapter Four: Why Men Won't Commit

There's a general perception among a lot of people that men won't commit. Now, while there are many men who would really like to stay away from commitment in relationships as much as possible, there are also many others out there who are ready and willing to commit once they have found the right person to commit to . For most men, it's not the idea of commitment that is scary and daunting, but rather the prospect of failing, or committing to the wrong person, and then being unable to get out of the situation or having to deal with the consequences.

Now, if you are already married you have obviously already passed the stage where your man is afraid of commitment in that sense, but for those who are in relationships but not married yet (and in long-term relationships at that), there may be some commitment issues at play that need to be addressed. This is especially problematic if you have already made it very clear to your boyfriend or partner that you are ready to take the relationship to the next level and have a more serious commitment, such as marriage or living together, but the man is not ready to take the leap just yet.

Before you figure out some reasons why your man won't commit long-term, you also have to consider whether he is actually going to commit in the first place. How sure are you that this man you have been seeing or hanging out with for a few months is actually in it for the long haul? For men, if they are interested in a long-term committed relationship with you, they will let you know and you will get very clear signals.

There are also signals you will get if they are not interested in anything long-term. If the guy will not introduce you to his family, for instance, then most likely he doesn't see the need for you to get to know his family or connect with them because he doesn't see a future with you. This may be different if he is estranged from his family, but if he has that one older brother he is really close to and he has yet to introduce you, then he very likely isn't looking for a commitment.

It's not enough for the man to just introduce you to his friends, because for a lot of guys it's not really that big of a deal. However, if your boyfriend or partner won't introduce you to his friends, or tries to avoid the situation, you should also be very wary and just assume he is not going to commit any time soon. Perhaps he only thinks of you as someone he wants to see on the side, but without anyone else knowing. This is a definite signal that he will not commit to you.

Many women have heard the lines, "I'm not looking for a relationship right now" or "I don't want labels". When a man tells you this , it means he is not looking for a relationship with you and you should probably start moving on to something more serious. As already mentioned, if a man likes you and sees a future with you, he will definitely let you know of his intentions. Any vague declarations of indecisiveness or hesitation simply mean he doesn't see himself with you in the long run, so you should not hope for anything more either.

What keeps guys from committing? For many, it's other priorities such as school, work, or a business opportunity. If your boyfriend is graduating from business or law school and has a lot of transitions in his mind over the next year or so, he probably will not be ready for a long-term relationship until things settle down and he knows what he wants to do next. It's probably not because you are inadequate or not relationship material, but just the fact that he is preoccupied with so many other things and has a lot on his plate at the moment.

Now, if a man has so many big things coming up and he is making sure to include you in every part of it, *don't let go of him.* He is planning his future and he is including you in it. He wants to experience what it is like to attain success in his career or business goals with you in his arms. He wants to end the day with you, and celebrate those milestones with you. He is in it for the long haul, and you will definitely see him going out of his way to make your relationship work, no matter the cost.

On the other hand, if he disappears from your radar for days or weeks at a time, and then pops back up as if nothing happened or it's not a big deal, take it as a sign that you are not his priority and he is just focused on other things at this time. This is not wrong in and of itself; in fact, this may be your arrangement all along, and as long as both parties are clear about the lack of expectations, then that is up to you. But if you are holding out for him and he is not even showing you any signs of interest, then you are selling yourself short.

Some men are unwilling to commit because they have had bad experiences in past relationships and may not be ready to jump in again. This is normal even for women, but can also become a cop-out later on for men who just want the benefits without any strings attached. There may have been bad experiences with past relationships, but if a man sees someone whom he sees as the right person for him, he will definitely make the effort to connect with that person and plan a future together.

Are you seeing a guy at the moment who says he likes spending time with you but without labels because of a bad relationship in the past? This is unfair to you because you are not in any way responsible for what has transpired to him in the past. The more likely possibility is he just wants to play around, or is just lonely and looking for companionship, but if he is not taking the next step with you then he doesn't see himself with you in the coming years, and you shouldn't expect too much either.

Men are not as verbal as women, generally speaking, but men are also not as veiled or indirect when it comes to their actions. This means if you are looking for a serious, long-term commitment and he is giving you vague generalities or avoiding the next step altogether, then you are better off looking somewhere else. Once the male has found a suitable mate, he will let that female know. All other indications and insinuations that are not quite there mean exactly that - you're not the woman he is looking for, so he's not going to commit.

Assess where you are in your relationship at the moment. Who is putting in more of the effort between you and the guy? Are you constantly the one who arranges for you and your boyfriend or partner to have dinner together or spend time together? Remember, if the guy is really interested in you, he will initiate contact with you. He will want to spend time with you no matter how busy you both may be. Men are hunters by nature, and they will be persistent about it, circling their prey and enjoying the thrill of the hunt. But if you are the one doing the hunting, and he always seems to try to wiggle out of spending time with you, don't expect him to be having the talk with you any time soon.

More than likely, if this is where you're at in your current relationship, he's just waiting for someone better to come along, then he'll be ready to ditch you. It may seem blunt or unfair, but that is how it has transpired for so many women in this kind of situation, so you would do well to sit up and take notice. If he is not showing interest now, he probably won't down the road, and a real, lasting commitment and connection with this man is out of the question.

Chapter Five: Why Men Lose Interest

Monotony is the bane of any relationship. No matter how much you love someone and how much you enjoy doing things together, when everything becomes a routine and monotony sets in, you will begin to lose interest and notice that passion slowly fading away. This is why relationship experts and marriage counselors advise couples to always find ways to spice up their relationship and explore new activities together.

Both men and women can lose interest in a relationship, but for different reasons because of the way men and women are wired. For instance, a woman can get tired of having to wait for a man to commit or become more assertive in the relationship, or she may give up having to deal with her in-laws who are constantly trying to influence their relationship. For the man, interest can be lost when he feels that his personal worth is no longer recognized in the relationship.

One of the most common ways men lose interest is when they are no longer the hunter, or they feel that too much attention is coming from the woman they are interested in only pursuing on a shallow level. The man likes the thrill of chasing after the woman he is interested in, but if he is only interested in a sexual tryst, for instance, and the the female immediately exhibits too much flattery towards him, the average man would steer clear.

The example above usually happens in the dating scene, however, and for those already in a relationship, there are other factors at play. In general, men are very particular about their hobbies and recreational activities, whether this is golf or tennis on Saturdays, video game nights with their buddies, monster truck shows or rodeo performances on Sundays, or their miniature train collection. Men see these activities as their way to let off steam, relax their minds, and let loose with their friends after all responsibilities are taken care of.

Now, if the woman begins to lay down unreasonable rules or demands that encroach on the man's private time and his ability to enjoy some activities on his own, this could cause not just tension but a waning interest in pursuing the relationship further. Some women insist that their husband or boyfriend accompany them to the outlet mall, or the latest chick flick, but get irritated and act all jealous or clingy when the guy wants to hang out with his friends and do guy stuff. Inevitably, the man will get tired and move on.

Sexual compatibility is yet another factor consider when figuring out why a man has lost interest, or is drifting away. Keep in mind that humans are wired to reproduce sexually, and the man is looking for a potential mate to have children with, but if there is no sexual chemistry from the get-go or it is lost somewhere in the middle of the relationship period, things can start to go downhill.

It may sound like a trivial matter on paper, but for the vast majority of people sexual compatibility is way up there in the priority list when considering whether someone is to be considered as a long-term prospect. Perhaps you get along with this guy so well, you share many interests, and you have very identical goals in life. Once he finds out you are sexually compatible, this is a major plus for both of you. But if he realizes your sexual energy or physical chemistry do not match, it may cause him to lose interest or even just slowly disappear from the scene. Sad as it may be, this is true for many relationships and must be understood as part of how men are wired to procreate.

Unfortunately, another reason why a man would lose interest is if he has already found someone who has captured his attention and makes him feel wanted again. As discussed in previous chapters, men are looking for an emotional affirmation or intimacy with their partner. If they are not getting it from their wife or girlfriend, they are vulnerable to the intimacy or emotional connection offered by others around them, and when this happens their attention gravitates towards the new source of emotional happiness, while drifting from the current relationship.

At times, it really just boils down to the excitement factor. Now, it is true that a relationship is a commitment, and it must be honored as a partnership between two parties who must work together to maintain the bond they have shared. In a marriage, there is an actual legally binding contract in place that both the man and the woman must honor, and there is no justification for drifting away or checking out of the relationship because the excitement of the first few months or years is no longer there.

But who can blame them for wanting out when the relationship is all but exciting? This is when it is necessary for an emotional intimacy to be established again, because only honest, transparent communication between the two partners will be able to restore what was lost. For the woman, in particular, who is struggling to understand why her male counterpart has lost interest, a careful and balanced self-assessment may be necessary but without self-blaming or laying all the guilt on your part.

What elements of your relationship would benefit from a major overhaul or a reimagining? It may be something as simple as trying new restaurants on your free nights, or experimenting with new sexual positions or techniques in bed. Perhaps a change of social scenery is due? Ask your spouse or partner if he really enjoys hanging out with your friends from the book club every Wednesday night, or if he would rather go bowling and invite your other couple friends.

As a woman, you should know that men are, for the most part, quite easy to negotiate with. A simple compromise goes a long way with your man, and frankly, if your relationship has gone on for a long time (two years or longer) and he already knows you very well, he is all too willing to negotiate and compromise with you anyway. Alternate between activities that you both like, and decide on things you both would like to try, and you will notice how much easier it will be to negotiate with your man on other things.

A man who really loves you will, at the end of the day, just want to spend time with you. But how much more enjoyable and memorable would it be for him if it was doing something or going somewhere he actually enjoys? Surprise him one time by offering to join him and his buddies for one of their poker sessions, for instance. If he has already invited you to this a long time ago, but you've always turned him down, watch the excitement in his eyes the moment you bring it up, not to mention the pride on his face when he walks into that poker room with you in his arms. This would probably be the perfect time for you to mention that new California king you wanted to purchase, by the way (he'll be in such a good mood he'll probably buy two if you insist).

A relationship is a two-way street, and it is up to both of you to keep the fire alive. Your role as the woman is to make it clear to your spouse, partner, or boyfriend that his interest also matter, and that you are willing to try new things with him. After all, when you chose to be in a relationship with him, this also meant understanding his many facets and quirks, strengths and weaknesses, because you wanted to know who he truly is as a person.

Don't allow monotony to set in and become a dark cloud over the relationship you have already nurtured together. When you find yourself in a rut, simply go back to how it was when you first met each other. Remember how passionate and excited you were to see each other, and how you could not wait to be in each other arms even if it were just for a few moments? The reason for this excitement is the newness of it all, the excitement of getting to know someone and finding out what makes them happy.

Do you know everything about your spouse or boyfriend already? Most likely, regardless of how long you have been together, there are still a lot of things you have not discovered about him. Why not make it your daily decision to find out more about him every day and keep the passion alive? When you are always discovering your partner, it won't get boring because you see a new aspect of his personality each time.

Chapter Six: How To Avoid Rejection From Men

So you talked to this guy, shared some stories, and he seemed quite interested in getting to know you. You exchanged phone numbers and he said he will call you sometime, but he never did. What just happened? It's not like you did anything wrong (or maybe you did?) that would have turned him off, right?

Because men are seen mostly as the initiators in our society, there is a lot of discussion about turning down men or letting them down easy. But we also have to talk about how to avoid rejection coming from men, which does happen quite frequently as well, especially for women who are single and in the dating scene.

Now, what you should realize first of all is despite all of their attempts to look all strong, confident, and assertive, men also battle a lot of insecurities and fears of their own. If you are hesitant about approaching or starting a conversation with a man you are interested in, men are just as petrified of talking to you or a woman they have had their eyes on. It's a normal human emotion, the fear of rejection.

We are scared of rejection because, well, it's embarrassing especially if it happens in front of a lot of people. Worse, if it happens in front of your friends or people you know from work. So the next time you are wondering why the guy is acting the way he is or seems uncomfortable, it may be because he is in front of people he knows and he is also afraid of rejection.

When men and women interact, they give off a lot of signals to each other indicating interest or attraction. For some, the chemistry is palpable the moment their eyes lock from across the room. The guy walks up and introduces himself, and sparks fly right away. It is not uncommon for a long conversation to ensue, followed by a nightcap somewhere else. A new relationship is born as two compatible people meet.

For most, the first meeting may have the same tension when eye contact is first made, but the hesitation sets in when it comes time to actually initiate conversation. *What if he is already taken? What if he is not really interested, or if it's my friend he actually likes?* These questions are all too real, and they get even more daunting as you play them over and over in your head while deciding whether to approach the guy or not.

If you do decide to approach the guy or just raise the ante and send him some not-so-subtle hints such as sending some drinks over to his table, be careful not to overdo the overtures or display too much enthusiasm. Just a tease or a sneak peek would do, but don't lay all your cards on the table just yet. Send the drinks to his table, acknowledge when he mouths 'Thank you', and then go back to talking to your friends as if you send drinks to tables all the time.

Now, watch what happens. If the guy approaches your table and introduces himself with a handshake and a smile, you've found yourself a true gentleman. This guy will do the right thing and approach the lady who just paid for his drink, and will have the decency to introduce himself, find out yours, and let you know he appreciates the attention. Does he like you? Too early to tell, but you got his attention and now the ball is in his court. What he does next, and how he acts in front of you, will help you determine if he is interested, but don't let him in too easy just yet. Guys like the challenge, so make him work for it.

The key to avoiding rejection from men is to not take away the challenge from them. They like the challenge, they live for it, and if you take it away from them they will lose interest and focus their attention somewhere else. There is nothing wrong with giving them some hints that you like them or are at least interested in them, but keep things vague at first. This also gives you time to gauge whether they are really into you or not, so you can lessen the risk of putting it all out there for a man only to get rejected.

Rejection doesn't just happen in the dating scene, but also within relationships. In particular, you would want to avoid some tried and tested behaviors that men dislike in women, such as incessant nagging or blaming. Because men are generally not verbal creatures, they tend to tune you out the moment you start an outburst about a mundane thing that can be resolved otherwise. If the nagging or finger-pointing become more frequent, your partner will soon tune out not just what you are saying, but from the relationship as a whole, and you just might find yourself out of the relationship not too long after.

Within the bounds of the relationship, mutual respect and clear lines of communication along with reasonable expectations are necessary to keep the connection pleasant, and also to minimize the risk of rejection or a bad ending to the relationship. Be on the lookout for those little things that, if left unresolved and allowed to continue, soon add up and have a drastic effect on your partnership.

On the other hand, if there is trouble on the horizon already and your partner or spouse asks for some space, it is better to give him that space to be able to think things through and clear his head. Men are different from women in that they find solace and clarity in being alone, whereas women would run to the company of loved ones or friends so they can spill their woes and hear what everyone has to tell them.

Men don't usually like clingy, needy types, and being all clingy when your man simply wants to be alone with his thoughts can be disastrous for your relationship, leading to rejection. Once he is ready to reconnect with you again, he will make the effort to do so. But don't make the mistake of getting in the way or hanging on to him when he needs his personal space. This is a sure recipe for rejection.

Not all men are control freaks, but men in general are very particular about being control of their romantic options (in the dating scene) and their personal space (for those in relationships). Whether you are interacting with a man in the dating environment, or navigating various relationship boundaries with a partner or spouse, take care not to seem too overbearing to him by attempting to take over the personal space where he feels most in control of his thoughts and feelings.

For men, when you are already tramping on what they have always regarded as their sacred ground or sanctuary, you become an adversary rather than an ally, and they will likely react in a territorial manner, acting out in rejection and causing further trouble. It is best for both parties to just simmer down, let cooler heads prevail, and allow for some calm, quiet thinking.

Conclusion

Thanks again for buying this book!

You should now have a good understanding of men, and be able to improve your love life.

Men may be hard to understand at times, but women just can't get enough of them anyway, right? You've probably sworn off guys in the past, especially after a particularly painful break-up or experience, but after a while you will find yourself interested again, ready to try one more time.

That is, after all, the essence of the human experience. You learn from your experiences, go through the hits and the misses, and must always be ready to get back right up and try again until you get it right.

In relationships with men, there's a lot of trial-and-error happening, so you really have to be flexible and open to different scenarios that could arise. This is especially true in today's modern society, where people's attention spans are much shorter and distractions abound everywhere. You will find yourself competing for the attention of your spouse or partner with other people, or even gadgets, games, career opportunities, and other attention-getters.

But let's be very honest here: while men may be difficult to comprehend, it is also what makes them the mysterious and intriguing creatures that they are, making them more attractive to the female gender. If men were just plain and simple robots you could program to your desired specifications and to cater to your every whim, it won't be long before you get tired of the lack of adventure.

For all their weaknesses, weird workings, and strange activities, men are compatible with women and they make for great spouses and partners, so don't count them off just yet. As a woman, you can learn so much and grow in character by simply attempting to understand the inner workings of the male psyche and how they are wired to protect you and procreate with you.

The feminist icon Anais Nin summarizes the intricate connection between men and women in her book *The Diary of Anais Nin:*

"Man can never know the loneliness a woman knows. Man lies in the woman's womb only to gather strength, he nourishes himself from this fusion, and then he rises and goes into the world, into his work, into battle, into art. He is not lonely. He is busy. The memory of the swim in amniotic fluid gives him energy, completion. Woman may be busy too, but she feels empty. Sensuality for her is not only a wave of pleasure in which she is bathed, and a charge of electric joy at contact with another. When man lies in her womb, she is fulfilled, each act of love a taking of man within her, an act of birth and rebirth, of child rearing and man bearing. Man lies in her womb and is reborn each time anew with a desire to act, to be. But for woman, the climax is not in the birth, but in the moment man rests inside of her."

Men and women need each other in this existence, so attempting to understand your partner's maleness need not be burdensome or daunting. Consider it a chance for you to better relate to this person whom you are devoting much of your time and energy to, and a worthy investment as you build a future together.

If you enjoyed this book, please take the time to leave me a review on Amazon. I appreciate your honest feedback, and it really helps me to continue producing high quality books.

Thanks!

Made in the USA
Columbia, SC
30 October 2019